THE SHADOW

HANS CHRISTIAN ANDERSEN

(FROM _HANS ANDERSEN FORTY-TWO STORIES_ [1930],
TRANSLATED BY M. R. JAMES)
[ZHINGOORA BOOKS]

This edition is published by
Zhingoora Books.

The Cover is Designed by Pallav Sethiya.

Hans Christian Andersen was born on 2nd April 1805 and died on 4th August 1875. He was a Danish author, writer and poet. His famous works are "The Steadfast Tin Soldier," "The Snow Queen," "The Little Mermaid," "Thumbelina," "The Little Match Girl," and "The Ugly Duckling.

In the hot countries the sun can burn properly. People become as brown as mahogany all over; in the very hottest countries they are even burnt into negroes—but it was only to the hot countries that a learned man from the cold ones had come. He imagined he would be able to run about as he did at home, but he soon got out of the habit of doing that. He and all sensible people had to stop indoors. The window-shutters and the doors were kept shut all day, and it looked as if the whole house were asleep or else nobody was at home. The narrow street with the tall houses, where he lived, was so built that from morning to night the sunshine lay on it; really it was unbearable. This learned man from the cold countries—he was a young man and a clever one—he felt as if he was living in a fiery furnace. It exhausted him, and he grew quite thin, and even his shadow contracted and got much smaller than it was at home; the sun exhausted it, too. Not until evening, when the sun was down, did they begin to revive.

That, now, was really a pleasure to see. As soon as lights were brought into the room the Shadow stretched itself all up the wall—yes, up to the ceiling, too, so long did it make itself, for it had to stretch itself to get its strength back. The learned man went out on the balcony, to stretch himself there, and as the stars came out in the lovely clear sky he seemed to himself to be coming to life again.

On all the balconies in the street—and in the hot countries every window has a balcony—people came out, for air one must have, even if one's accustomed to be the colour of mahogany. Very lively it became—upstairs and downstairs. Shoemakers and tailors and everybody else moved out into the street; tables and chairs were brought out and lamps lit—thousands of them—and some talked and others sang; and the people took walks, and the carriages drove out, and the donkeys with bells on them went by—"Kling-a-ling-a-ling!" There were funerals, with singing of psalms; the street-boys fired off throw-downs; the church bells rang out, and altogether it was very lively down in the street. Only in one house, straight opposite to that in which the foreign learned man lived, was there complete stillness. And yet somebody lived in it, for there were flowers on the balcony, that grew splendidly in the hot sun, which they couldn't have done without being watered, and there must be somebody to water them; so there must be people there. The door of it, too, was opened at night, but inside it was quite dark; at any rate in the front room. But from further in there was a sound of music. To the foreign scholar it seemed incomparably beautiful, but it might easily be that he fancied it so, for in the hot countries everything seemed to him matchless, but for the heat. The landlord said he didn't know who had taken the house opposite, for you couldn't see any people, and as for the music, he thought it horribly tiresome. "It's like someone sitting practising a piece he can't get on with—always the same piece. No doubt he's saying, 'I shall get it right in time', but he won't get it right, however long he goes on playing."

One night the foreign scholar woke up. The door to the balcony stood open where he slept and the curtain before it was lifted by the breeze, and he thought there was a marvellous light coming from the balcony opposite. All the flowers were shining like flames of the most lovely colours, and among the flowers stood a slender, graceful maiden; herself, too, shining, as it seemed. It positively dazzled his eyes, and he shut them as tight as ever he could, and woke up completely. With a single jump he was on the floor, and very quietly he stole behind the curtain, but the maiden was gone, the light was gone, the flowers shone no longer, though they stood there as fair as ever. The door was ajar, and from far within the music was sounding, soft and beautiful; such as would entrance one into delicious thought. It really was like magic—and who was it that lived there? Where was the proper entrance? The whole ground floor was a succession of shops, and people couldn't always be passing through them.

One evening the foreign scholar was sitting out on his balcony, and a lamp was hung in the room behind him, and so it very naturally happened that his shadow passed across to the wall opposite, and there it stayed, right opposite among the flowers on the balcony, and when the learned man moved the shadow moved, too—it always does.

"I think my Shadow is the only living thing to be seen over there," said the learned man. "Look how snug it's sitting among the flowers, and the door's standing ajar. Now if only the Shadow was sharp enough to go in and look about and then come and tell me what it saw! Yes, you'd be some use then," he said in joke. "Do, please, go in there! Do! Are you going?" With that he nodded to the Shadow, and the Shadow nodded back. "Well, go then, but don't stay away!" The learned man got up and his Shadow, on the balcony opposite, got up too. The learned man turned, and the Shadow turned too, and if anyone had been observing carefully, they would have seen, quite plain, that the Shadow went in by the half-open door of the balcony over the way, at the moment when the learned man went into his own room and let fall the long curtain behind him.

Next morning the learned man went out to take his coffee and read the papers. "What's this?" he said, when he came out into the sunshine. "I haven't got any shadow! Why, then it really did go away last night and has not come back; that's rather tiresome, that is."

It did annoy him, but not so much because his shadow was gone, as because he knew that there was a story about a man without a shadow which everyone at home in the cold countries knew; and if the learned man went there and told them his own story they would say he was merely imitating the other, and that he had no business to do. So he determined to say nothing at all about it, which was very sensible of him.

In the evening he went out on to his balcony again; he had put the lamp behind him, very properly, for he knew that a shadow always needs its master for a screen, but he couldn't entice it back. He made himself little and he made himself big, but no shadow came, nobody came. He coughed loudly, but it was no good.

It was amazing, to be sure; but in those hot countries everything grows very fast, and after a week had passed he saw, to his great delight, that a new shadow was growing out of his feet when he went into the sunlight: the root must have been left behind. In three weeks' time he had a very tolerable shadow, which, when he betook himself home to the northern country, grew more and more on the way, so that at last it was so long and so big that he would have been contented with half as much.

So the learned man came home and wrote books about what there was of truth and goodness and beauty in the world; and days passed by, and years—many years.

He was sitting in his room one evening, and there came a very gentle knock at the door. "Come in!" said he; but nobody came in, so he opened the door, and there standing before him was an extraordinarily thin man, so thin as to be quite remarkable. This person was, for the rest, extremely well dressed, and evidently a man of distinction.

"Whom have I the honour of addressing?" asked the learned man.

"Ah, I thought very likely you wouldn't recognize me," said the well-dressed man. "I've become so much of a body that I've actually got flesh and clothes; you never expected to see me in such fine condition. Don't you recognize your old shadow? To be sure, you certainly never thought I should ever come back. Things have gone wonderfully well with me since I was with you last, and I have become very well-to-do in every respect. If I wish to buy myself out of service, I have the means." And he rattled a large bunch of valuable seals that hung to his watch, and put his hand to the heavy gold chain that was round his neck: and how his fingers did glitter with diamond rings, and all real too!

"Well, well! I can't get over it," said the learned man. "What does it all mean?"

"I admit, it's by no means an ordinary affair," said the Shadow. "But, then, you yourself are not an ordinary man; and I, as you very well know, have trod in your footsteps from a child. As soon as you found that I was ripe to go out into the world by myself, I went my own way. I am now in the most brilliant circumstances, but there came a sort of longing over me to see you once more before you die, as die you must. I wanted, too, to see this part of the world again, for one has always a fondness for one's Fatherland. I am aware that you have got another shadow in my place; if I have anything to pay, either to it or to you, I hope you will be so good as to let me know."

"Well, and is it really you?" said the scholar. "It is indeed most remarkable! I could never have believed that my old shadow could come back to me as a man."

"Do tell me what I have to pay," said the Shadow; "I don't at all like to be in debt of any kind."

"How can you talk so?" said the learned man. "What debt is there to talk of? Be as free as the next man; I am extraordinarily pleased at your good fortune. Do sit down, old friend, and just tell me a little about how it all came about, and what you saw at the house over the way, out there in the hot country."

"I will tell you," said the Shadow, seating himself; "but you must promise me that you won't tell anyone here in the town, wherever you may meet me, that I was once your Shadow. I have some thoughts of becoming engaged. I could support more families than one."

"Be quite easy," said the scholar; "I won't tell anyone who you really are. Here's my hand on it. I promise it, and one man, one word, you know." "One word, one shadow," said the Shadow; he was obliged to phrase it so.

It was indeed most remarkable to see how much of a man the Shadow was: all dressed out in the finest possible black broadcloth, with varnished boots and a hat that would shut up so that it was only crown and brim, not to speak of what we know already, the seals, the gold chain, and the diamond rings. The Shadow was, in fact, extraordinarily well dressed, and this was just what made him a complete man.

"Now I'll tell you my story," said the Shadow, planting his feet, in the varnished boots, as firmly as he could on the arm of the learned man's new shadow, which lay at his feet like a poodle dog: and this was either out of pride or perhaps in hopes of getting it to stick to him; while the prostrate shadow kept very quiet in order to listen, for it wanted to know how a shadow could get free as this one had done, and work up to be its own master.

"Do you know who it was that lived in the house over the way?" said the Shadow. "It was the most beautiful thing there is: it was Poetry. I was there for three weeks, and the effect was the same as if one had spent three thousand years in reading everything that has been sung and written. I say it, and it is the truth. I have seen everything, and I know everything."

"Poetry!" cried the learned man. "Yes! Yes! She often dwells, a hermit, in great cities. Poetry! I saw her for one single brief moment, but my eyes were full of sleep. She was standing on the balcony and shining as the Northern Lights shine. Tell me, tell me of her. Thou wast on the balcony, thou wentest through the door, then——" "Then I was in the ante-room," said the Shadow. "You were always sitting looking across at the ante-room. There was no light there at all; there was a sort of twilight, but one door stood open, leading straight to a second, and into a long row of rooms and halls. There was light there. I should have been killed outright by the light, had I gone in to where the maiden was, but I was careful, I gave myself time—as indeed one must."

"And what sawest thou then?" asked the scholar.

"I saw everything, and I will tell you about it. But—it isn't that I'm in the least proud—but considering I'm a free man, and what accomplishments I possess, not to mention my good position and my very easy circumstances—I should very much prefer you to address me as 'you'."

"I beg your pardon," said the scholar; "it's merely old habit which sticks by me. You're perfectly right, and I shall keep it in mind. But now, do tell me everything you saw."

"Everything!" said the Shadow. "For I saw everything and I know everything."

"What was it like in the innermost hall?" asked the scholar. "Was it like being in the green wood? Was it like a solemn temple? Were the halls like the starlit sky seen from the top of the high mountains?" "Everything was there," said the Shadow; "I didn't go absolutely in, I stayed in the room next to it in the twilight, but I was admirably placed, and saw everything and know everything.

I have been in the court of Poetry, in the ante-chamber."

"But what did you see? Did all the gods of ancient days pass through the vast halls? Did the heroes of old times fight their battles there? Were there lovely children playing and telling of their dreams?"

"I tell you I was there, and you may imagine I saw everything there was to be seen. Had you been over there you would not have turned into a man, but I did; and, moreover, I learned to know my innermost nature, all that was inborn in me, the kinship I had with Poetry. When I was with you I never thought about it, but, as you know, every time the sun rose or set I used to become amazingly large. In the moonlight, indeed, I was almost plainer to be seen than you yourself. At that time I did not comprehend my own nature, but in that ante-room it became clear to me; I became a man. When I came out I was matured, but you were no longer in the hot countries. I was ashamed, as a man, to go about as I was. I needed boots and clothes and all the human paraphernalia that make a man recognizable. I made my way (I tell you this, you won't put it in a book), I made my way to the cake-woman's skirt, and hid myself under it. Little did the woman think how great a thing she had in hiding, and not till the evening did I come out. I ran along the street in the moonlight. I stretched myself right up the wall (it tickles one in the back deliciously). I ran up, I ran down; I peeped through the topmost windows, into the rooms, on to the roof. I peeped where no one else could, and saw what nobody else saw, and what nobody was meant to see. Take it all round, the world's a mean place. I wouldn't have become a man if it hadn't been generally assumed that it's a good thing to be one. I saw the most incredible things, among wives, among husbands, among parents and among those darling admirable children. I saw", said the Shadow, "what no human being was allowed to know, but what everybody very much wants to know, that is their neighbours' wrongdoings. If I'd written a newspaper it would have been read, I tell you! But I wrote direct to the people concerned, and there was a panic in every town I visited. They were terribly afraid of me, and they became amazingly fond of me. The professors made me a professor, the tailors gave me new clothes. I'm admirably fitted out. The master of the mint coined money for me, and the women said I was very good-looking. In this way I became the man I am. And now I must bid you good-bye. Here's my card; I live on the sunny side, and I'm always at home when it rains." And off went the Shadow.

"That is a most remarkable affair," said the learned man.

A year and a day passed, and the Shadow came again. "How goes it?" he asked.

"Alas!" said the learned man. "I write about the true and the good and the beautiful. But nobody cares to hear about such things, and I'm quite in despair. I feel it very keenly."

"But I don't," said the Shadow; "I'm getting fat and that's what everybody ought to try to be. You don't understand the way of the world, you know; you'll get quite ill like this, you ought to travel. I'm going to travel this summer; will you come with me? I should like to have a companion; will you go with me as my shadow? It'll be a real pleasure to have you with me, and I'll pay expenses."

"That's going a bit too far," said the learned man.

"Why, that's as you take it," said the Shadow. "It'll do you all the good in the world to travel. If you'll be my shadow you shan't have a penny to pay for the trip."

"That's absolute madness!" said the learned man.

"But after all, the world's like that," said the Shadow, "and so it always will be." And off he went.

The learned man was in a bad way: sorrow and trouble were on him, and as for his talk about the true and the beautiful and the good, most people appreciated it as a cow does roses. At last he became quite ill. "You really look like a shadow," people said to him; and the learned man shivered, for it was exactly what he was thinking.

"You ought to take some baths," said the Shadow, who paid him a visit. "There's nothing else for it. I'll take you with me for old acquaintance sake. I'll pay expenses, and you shall write a description and amuse me with it on the journey. I'm going to the baths, for my beard won't grow as it should, and that is an ailment; one must have a beard. Now do be reasonable and accept my invitation; we'll travel as friends."

So they set off. The Shadow was the master and the master was the shadow. They drove together, they rode and walked together side by side or in front or behind, according as the sun shone. The Shadow was always careful to keep in the master's place, and the learned man didn't really think much about that; he was a very good soul, extremely kind and friendly. And so one day said he to the Shadow: "As we've become travelling companions (as we are) and as we've grown up together from childhood, wouldn't it be nice to drink brotherhood, and call each other 'thou'. It's more sociable, isn't it?"

"Now you're talking," said the Shadow (who was in fact the master). "What you say is very frank and very well meant. I'll be equally frank and well meaning. You as a scholar know very well what an odd thing Nature is. Some people can't bear to touch brown paper, it makes them sick; others feel it all over their body when someone scratches a pane of glass with a nail. Now I get just that sensation when I hear you say 'thou' to me. I feel absolutely as if I were crushed down on the ground, as I was in my first situation with you. You understand, it's merely a sensation, not pride at all. I can't bear you saying 'thou' to me, but I'll gladly say 'thou' to you; and that's meeting you halfway."

So the Shadow addressed his former master as "thou".

"Upon my word, it's rather much," thought the learned man, "that I should have to say 'you' and he should say 'thou'." But he had to put up with it.

Eventually they came to a watering-place where there were a number of visitors, and among them a beautiful Princess, who was suffering from the complaint of seeing too well; which is, of course, very distressing.

She noticed at once that the newcomer was a very different sort of person from all the rest. "People say he has come here to get his beard to grow, but I can see the real reason. He can't cast a shadow."

Her curiosity was roused, and very soon she got into conversation with the strange gentleman, on the promenade. Being a Princess, she did not need to beat about the bush, so she said: "What's the matter with you is that you can't cast a shadow."

"Your Royal Highness must be considerably better," said the Shadow. "I am aware that your complaint is that you see too well; but it has yielded, and you are cured. I have, in fact, a quite unusual shadow. Do you see the person who always goes about with me? Other people have an ordinary shadow, but I don't care about what is ordinary. You give your servant finer clothes for his livery than you wear yourself, and just so I have had my shadow smartened up into a man. What's more, you can see that I have even given him a shadow. It costs money, but I do like to have something peculiar to myself."

"What!" thought the Princess. "Can I really have recovered? These baths are the best that exist! Waters certainly have an amazing power in these days. Still, I shan't go away; it's becoming lively here. I have an extraordinary liking for that stranger. I only hope his beard won't grow, for he'll go away if it does."

In the evening the Princess and the Shadow danced together in the great ball-room. She was light, but he was lighter, and such a partner she had never had. She told him what country she came from, and he knew it; he had been there, but at a time when she was not at home. He had peeped in at windows, upstairs and downstairs, and seen one thing and another, and so he could answer the Princess's questions and give her information that quite astounded her. He must be the wisest man on earth, she thought, and she conceived the greatest respect for his knowledge; and when they danced together a second time she fell in love with him. Of this the Shadow was well aware, for she gazed at him as if she would see through him. Yet once again they danced together, and she was on the point of speaking out. But she was careful. She thought of her country and realm and the many people she had to govern. "Wise he is," she thought to herself; "and that is a good point. He dances beautifully, and that's another. But is his knowledge thorough? That's equally important; that must be sifted." So she began very gradually to put to him some of the very most difficult questions, things she couldn't have answered herself, and the Shadow pulled a very odd face.

"Can't you answer me that?" asked the Princess.

"That was part of my nursery lessons," said the Shadow. "I really believe my shadow there behind the door can answer that."

"Your shadow?" said the Princess. "That would be most remarkable."

"Well, I don't say for certain that he can," said the Shadow, "but I think it, seeing he has been following me and listening to me all these years—I do think it. But your Royal Highness will permit me to call your attention to the fact that he takes such pride in passing for a man, that if he's to be in the right temper (as he must be to answer properly), he must be treated exactly like a man." "I'm perfectly agreeable to that," said the Princess. So she went across to the learned man at the door and talked to him about the sun and the moon, and about human nature, both outward and inward, and he answered her most wisely and well.

"What a man must he be who has so wise a shadow!" thought she. "It would be a real blessing for my people and my realm if I chose him for my consort. I will!"

And very soon they were agreed, the Princess and the Shadow, but no one was to know of it till she got back to her own kingdom.

"No one, not even my shadow," said the Shadow, who had his own thoughts about the matter.

And now they were in the country over which the Princess ruled when she was at home.

"Listen, my good friend," said the Shadow to the learned man. "I am now become as fortunate and as powerful as anyone can be, and now I will do something special for you. You shall always live with me in the palace, and drive out with me in my royal coach, and you shall have a hundred thousand rix-dollars a year. But you must allow yourself to be called a shadow by everyone, you must never say that you were at one time a man, and once a year, when I sit on the balcony in the sunshine and allow myself to be looked at, you must lie at my feet as a shadow ought to do. I may as well tell you that I am going to marry the Princess. The wedding is to take place this evening."

"No, no! That is really too much," said the learned man. "I won't allow it. I won't do it! It's deceiving the whole country and the Princess too. I shall tell the whole story—that I am the man and you are the shadow; you're only dressed up."

"Nobody will believe it," said the Shadow. "Do be reasonable, or I shall call the guard."

"I shall go straight to the Princess," said the learned man. "But I shall go first," said the Shadow, "and you'll go to prison." And there he had to go, for the sentries obeyed the one whom they knew the Princess was to marry.

"You are all in a tremble," said the Princess, when the Shadow came into her room. "Has anything happened? You mustn't be ill to-night; we're going to be married."

"I have had the most terrible experience that can occur to anyone," said the Shadow. "Only think of it—to be sure, a poor shadow's brain isn't equal to the strain—only think, my shadow has gone mad! He believes that he is the man and that I—just think of it—am his shadow!"

"That is awful," said the Princess; "I hope he is shut up?"

"Indeed he is. I'm afraid he'll never get the better of it."

"Poor shadow," said the Princess; "it's most unfortunate for him. It would really be a kindness to rid him of his little bit of life: indeed, when I come to think of it, I do believe it is essential that he should be quite quietly put out of the way."

"It's really very hard!" said the Shadow. "He was a faithful servant to me," and with that he seemed to sigh.

"You are a noble character," said the Princess.

That evening the whole town was illuminated, and the cannons went off "Boom!" And the soldiers presented arms. It _was_ a wedding, to be sure! The Princess and the Shadow went out on the balcony to show themselves and receive one last "Hurrah!"

The learned man heard nothing of all this, for he had already been executed.

[End of *The Shadow* by Hans Christian Andersen, from *Hans Andersen Forty-Two Stories*, translated by M. R. James]

The End

Printed in Great Britain
by Amazon

41672592R00020